Covering All Grounds

From Birth to Maturity in God

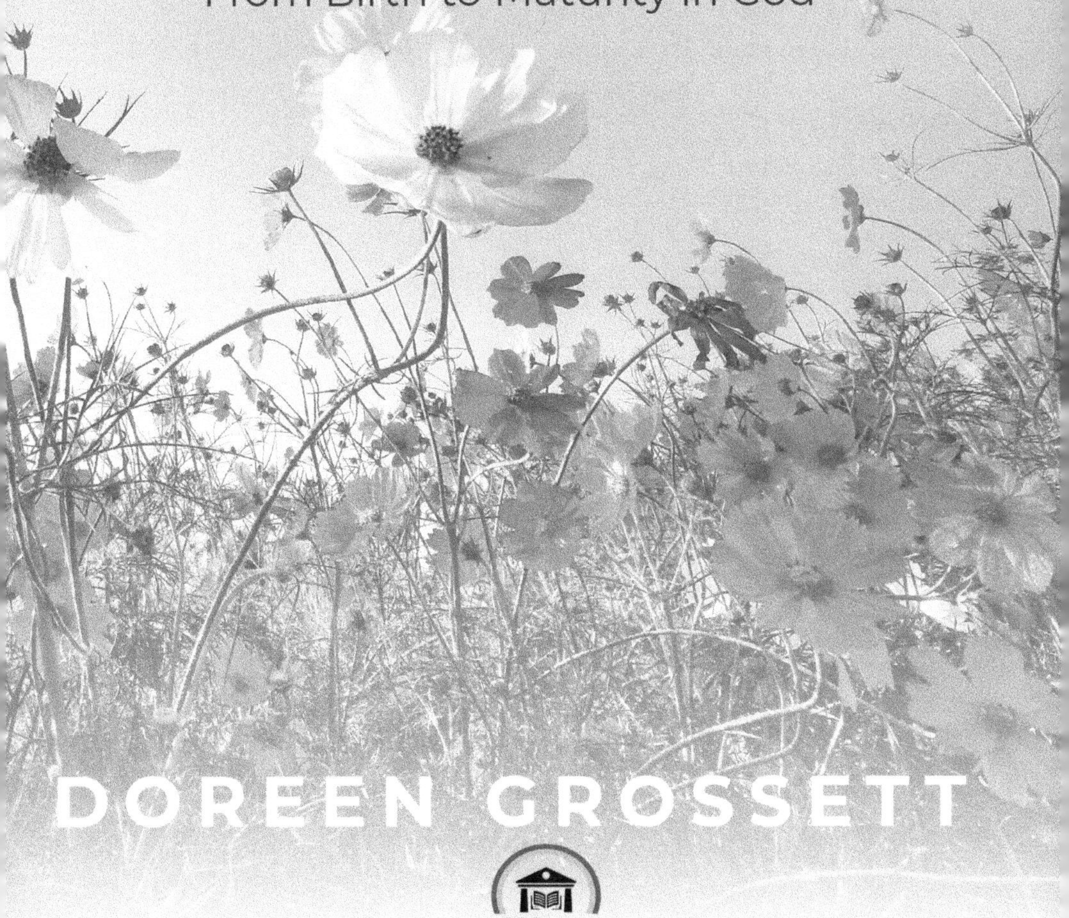

DOREEN GROSSETT

Copyright © 2024 by Doreen Grossett

All rights reserved. No part of this publication may be reproduced, distributed, or transmitted in any form or by any means, including, photocopying,recording, or other electronic or mechanical methods, without the prior written permission of the copyright owner and the publisher, except in the case of brief quotations embodied in critical reviews and certain other noncommercial uses permitted by copyright law. For permission requests, write to the publisher, addressed "Attention: Permissions Coordinator," at the address below.

ARPress
45 Dan Road Suite 5
Canton MA 02021
Hotline:				1(888) 821-0229
Fax:				1(508) 545-7580

Ordering Information:
Quantity sales. Special discounts are available on quantity purchases by corporations, associations, and others. For details, contact the publisher at the address above.

Printed in the United States of America.

ISBN-13:	Softcover	979-8-89389-531-5
	eBook	979-8-89389-532-2

Library of Congress Control Number: 2024920047

TABLE OF CONTENTS

CHAPTER ONE : THIS IS JUST THE BEGINNING.. 1

CHAPTER TWO : YOU ARE AN INFANT 5

CHAPTER THREE : DEVELOP AN APPETITE FOR THE WORD.............. 8

CHAPTER FOUR : THE IMPORTANCE OF THE HOLY SPIRIT............... 14

CHAPTER FIVE : SPRITUAL MATURITY 24

CHAPTER SIX : STRIVING FOR THE "ELECTUS"..................................... 29

CHAPTER SEVEN : KNOWING AND BELIEVING WHO YOU ARE........ 34

CHAPTER EIGHT : ENSURING YOUR SOUL IS AT PEACE 39

CHAPTER NINE : OUR OBLIGATION TO OTHERS................................. 43

CHAPTER TEN : YOU ARE EMPOWERED TO STAY "ON COURSE."..... 49

Chapter One:

THIS IS JUST THE BEGINNING

"In the beginning God created..."

Have you ever heard of the term, or have ever been told to, "start at the beginning?" If you have, what was the context in which it was said and why was it important that you do so?

Isn't it interesting how the two words have the same meaning, so that you are being told to "begin at the start" or "start at the beginning?"

In my childhood days at school, I can still remember how, during playtime, a group of us would compete with each other in foot races. These were usually impromptu – one member of the group would say, "Let us race", and the rest of us, with enthusiasm, would get down on our marks, get set, then ran off as fast as we could, each person striving to be the winner.

And, I can also remember that while we were running, other children would join us during the race and finish with us even though they had not been at the start of the race. There were times when they would even be the winner because they would join the race just ahead of us so that they could finish before us.

Of course, that was most unacceptable to the rest of us and we would vehemently protest, by telling them that they should "start at the beginning."

The Christian journey also has a beginning. The people who were witnesses to the apostles' Pentecostal Experience, asked of Peter and the rest of the disciples: "Men and brethren, what shall we do?" Peter told them that they should "start at the beginning."

Reading Peter's entire address to the crowd in Chapter 2 of Acts, we are able to understand the purpose and role of Jesus in man's redemption. Freshly anointed, Peter was able to explain it to them # while the Spirit of the Lord brought the conviction which led them to ask "how do we start?"

The response of Peter that they should "Repent, and be baptized every one of you in the name of Jesus Christ for the remission of sins, and ye shall receive the gift of the Holy Ghost" is the rejoicing of our hearts today because he went on to explain that this promise was unto them, and to their children, and to "all that are afar off", even as many as the Lord their God shall call.

Therefore, this promise is unto every one of us who desire to be reconciled unto God and we believe that it is through Jesus that it has been made possible. Jesus himself told Nicodemus in Chapter 3 of John that "God so loved the world; that he gave his only begotten Son, that 'whosoever' believeth in him should not perish, but have everlasting life. For God sent not his Son into the world to condemn the world; but that the world through him might be saved."

Every one of us who have met these criteria have embarked upon a journey that is both personal and individual. However, there is a very important thought that I wish to share with you my fellow sojourners and that is, as much as it is important to start at the beginning, it is equally important that we do not confuse the beginning of something with its ending. With so many years of life experiences under my belt, I have made the observation that people are, in many ways, "mistaking the beginning as the end."

Simply put, we are finishing where we should be starting. We are mistaking the "battle" for the "war" when the battle is only a part of the war – the war may consist of one or more battles. The battle that is won does not necessarily mean that the war is over. It is only a strategic success or an accomplished goal that is part of a bigger picture or a bigger objective, which is, to win the war.

This confusion of "mistaking the beginning as the end" is demonstrated in so many areas of our lives. Take for an example, the effort which a couple will put into their courtship and contrast it to the effort they put into their marriage.

Also, take note of how many people when they have achieved great successes very quickly, thereafter, have nothing to show for it; or the effort persons make to obtain their jobs but if you do a follow up three to six months after or even a year later their attitude is a complete right about.

But, the couple who put every effort into their courtship must now put even more effort into their marriage. Marriage, in their case, is only an important milestone. It is only one of their objectives in the relationship. Every couple who mistakes the marriage as an "end" goal will struggle in the marriage or fail at it.

The same is true of persons who work hard to achieve great success and later squander it because they fail to continue to do what is necessary to maintain that level of success or even to improve upon it.

How then can we, the people of God, learn from such an observation? How do we apply this learning to our own lives?

Well I have seen us, the people of God, making the same mistake in our Christian walk. We follow the word of God according to Acts 2:38 which says, "…. Repent, and be baptized every one of you in the name of Jesus Christ for the remission of sins, and ye shall receive the gift of the Holy Ghost….." yet, we fail to realize that this is only our first of many steps.

Think about it! We do behave as though the acceptance of Jesus Christ as our Lord and Savior is an accomplishment of itself and we are now eligible for eternal life. We say to ourselves mentally or act out the following: "Amen, Praise the Lord, I am done," or, "I can take it easy now, I just have to keep myself out of trouble and I am set for the Kingdom of God!"

This is a fundamentally wrong concept of Christians. We are certainly not done! Do you remember the story of the Prodigal Son? He is a very good example of someone "mistaking the beginning as the end." In his efforts to gain access to his inheritance, he failed to give due consideration to what he would do with it once he got it and the consequence or outcome attached to each of the choices he would make.

When his father handed him his inheritance, it was not the "end" but rather the "beginning." He was about to embark upon a journey that would take him back to his father in shame. He was about to learn a very painful lesson about "starting at the beginning" the hard way. The Prodigal Son needed to have heard someone say to him, when he received his inheritance, "this is just the beginning."

The same is true of when we accept Jesus Christ as our Savior. It is simply, yet significantly, a major milestone of our Christian journey. As the song says, "We've only just begun….."

What we are doing at this stage of our journey, is laying down the foundation on which we are about to build. In other words, we are doing our first works.

This is similar to purchasing a home or motor vehicle and knowing that we can only enjoy them for a long time with care and effort on our part. We must maintain them in very good condition for as long as we can or they will deteriorate and we lose them.

So it is with us. We immediately embark upon a journey when the Spirit of God ministers to us and stirs us to repentance, confession and baptism. But we have only just begun our journey to the Kingdom of God. This is a walk that is filled with pitfalls and challenges. It is a narrow road prescribed by Jesus but it is worthy of its destination.

We need not to be afraid for Jesus promises to be with us always. He has not asked us to walk where He himself has not walked. He is able to keep us from falling and to present us faultless before our Father.

It is a personal and individual walk but we walk in the company of others. Remember always that we walk in the company of angels for they are always encamped around us.

"Walk Good" is an expression used by Jamaicans to wish each other safe journey. We must take this walk! It is the walk of our lives! May we all "walk good" and "God speed" to all of us.

Chapter Two:

YOU ARE AN INFANT

"...As newborn babes desiring the sincere milk of the word...."

Oh yes, this is what we are when we first accept Christ and it is very important that we understand and accept that we are "babes" when we start out on our Christian journey.

The word of God describes us as babes which is an appropriate description given the fact that we have been born by water baptism.

This is in reference to a spiritual birth, hence, the scriptures' description of us is as "spiritual babes." Chapter 3 of I Corinthians also refers to us being fed with milk like babes.

What do we know about infants (babes) and what are the similarities we share with them? Well, let us look at some important facts about them.

Infants are completely dependent on others for care and assistance. They are incapable of doing anything for themselves at first. I have observed how the newborn is not able to focus its sight at birth but can do so after two weeks.

Infants do not know anything and are incapable of making decisions. In fact they are not required or expected to do so. We know the infant's limitations and match our expectations accordingly.

Infants take time to develop motor skills, eat with little assistance and learn how to communicate. They develop from using crying to communicate to speaking the language of their birth.

The most significant learning we can draw from the evolution of the infant through the different stages of development, is that there are some skills and abilities which come very quickly and that there are others that take a much longer time to develop.

Also, it is observed that each infant is unique in its individual development even while having the different aspects of that development in common with every baby.

When we consider the relationship and interaction of Jesus with his disciples we get glimpses of the different stages of their individual development. They were called together; they had the same access to Jesus; they were witnesses to the miracles and wonders of Jesus; yet the benefit to each was different in some ways even while they were enjoying the common benefits.

Understanding ourselves in the context of an infant's experience serves to make us humble about our calling of salvation. Herein is the integrity of God towards us. He knows we are new to this way of life. He knows it is "…not in man to do good…" and so he designs our transformation to take place over time.

This is exemplified in the Potter taking his time to develop a lump of clay into a useful vessel. The Potter does not immediately transform the clay into what he has in his mind. He must first remove all impurities from the clay; knead the clay like dough adding water to make it more pliable.

By the time the clay is placed on the wheel, it has already gone through a preparation process. Yet, it is still not ready for the fire (kiln). The lump of clay must now be molded by the potter into a useful vessel to his satisfaction.

Is the clay, which is now made into a vessel, ready for the fire? Not yet! The potter places it aside to sit for a while where it is allowed to dry and get hardened (tough). Now it is ready for the fire where it is transformed into a solid vessel. The final step in this process is the glazing of the outside of the vessel in order to seal it.

So it is in our development as Christian babes. We go through stages for development as we mature in the Lord. There are specific indicators which we look for in babies as they develop. These indicate if the infant is progressing well and if it is not, the necessary intervention is made. It is important for us to understand this so that we can align our expectations of ourselves as new converts with the word of God.

The thought I want to share with you on this topic is that you should not be too hard on yourself when you start your walk. Learn to creep before you walk. Enjoy your milk stage and grow strong in the Lord.

We observe the infant trying to take its first few steps and falling over and over again. Let us respond to our own failings as Christians, with the same patience we would exercise with an infant.

Chapter 2 of I John says, "My little children, these things write I unto you, that ye sin not. And if any man sin, we have an advocate with the Father, Jesus Christ the righteous:" We are both admonished and encouraged in this passage of scripture. We are admonished to "sin not" and encouraged to "seek the forgiveness of the Father through Jesus Christ our advocate if we do.

This is very important, because when we start our walk and fail sometimes, as we will, our failures can be used to discourage us or, an occasion for the "Accuser of the Brethren" to try to make us give up on ourselves.

Only Jesus was able to walk this journey without sin and He is well able to keep us in our own walk. Not in our own perfection nor in our own strength because we cannot; but in his, because when we sin, it is not held against us as long as we confess, repent and ask the Father for forgiveness through Jesus Christ.

It is the efficacious blood of our Jesus which makes our forgiveness possible and our walk a perfect one. The perfection of our walk is possible only in Jesus Christ. Jesus also helps us by providing a way of escape for us when we are tempted to do wrong.

Remember, when we start our Christian walk we are spiritual babes, limited in many areas of our lives. Spiritual expectations of us are according to our stages of development. We must therefore strive to grow in the word and in the grace of God through our Lord Jesus Christ.

Chapter Three:

DEVELOP AN APPETITE FOR THE WORD

"It is written, man shall not live by bread alone, but by every word..."

Are you one of those children who was fortunate or unfortunate to have a parent who forced you to eat your vegetables? Yes, it would be either fortunate or not, depending on your adult feelings on the matter. Or, was it something else that you just did not like to eat but you had to sit at the table until you ate it all? Remember how it felt like you were being punished?

How do you feel about it now that you are an adult and know that vegetables are good for you? I remember liking only tomatoes and nothing else: no carrots; lettuce; cucumbers; or any nothing else. No, not for me, and I can also remember the fights I had with my aunt over eating them.

Now, as an adult I eat them all and I am quite surprised at how much I like to eat vegetables. I have developed quite an appetite for them.

This experience of ours provides me with an opportunity to lay the foundation for sharing with you my thoughts about "developing an appetite for the word."

Our parents forced us to eat what they thought was good for us and they did it in our best interest. They had the authority to decide and exercised it accordingly. This, however, is not our God's approach in getting us to read his words. We are encouraged to do so, but he does not force us to do it. It is up to us to develop our own appetite for his word.

Now, consider the words of Jesus that "It is written, man shall not live by bread alone, but by every word..." to the devil at their first recorded encounter. Chapter 4 of Matthew narrates the entire exchange between them and it is important that we carefully note how this encounter was staged just after Jesus had completed 40 days of fasting.

What is evident to me, is the mentality of the devil in thinking that after 40 days of fasting Jesus would be so hungry and physically weak that he would be vulnerable to his "wiles" or tricks.

The first thought I would like to present to you is that throughout this encounter, the devil was careful to appeal to the three aspects of man's weakness:

(a) The lust of the flesh by recommending that Jesus turn the stones into bread;

(c) The lust of the eyes by showing Jesus all the of the worlds he could give him;

(c) The pride of life by daring him to show his power with the angels of God.

Jesus had put off his robe of divinity and was now clothed in flesh. He was now subject to temptation just as we are. By the devil's calculation, Jesus as flesh, was now, no different from us and therefore vulnerable to him and his temptation. The second thought I would like to present to you is the strategic use of the word of God by the Devil in his encounter with Jesus. Note how he said... "...he shall give his angels charge over thee .... lest thou dash thy foot against a stone." This is a direct quote from Chapter 91 of The Psalms. The devil knows the word of God and his boldness in using it in his attempt to persuade Jesus to obey him is an indication of the length to which he will go to derail us.

The third thought I would like to present to you is that Jesus was more than equipped to respond to the devil in using the word of God. In each exchange Jesus demonstrated for our benefit, the importance of an in-depth knowledge of the word of God.

Chapter 10 of Romans says "So then faith cometh by hearing, and hearing by the word of God." Our entire faith is based upon the word of God. It underpins everything we believe about God. Without the word of God, there would be no knowledge of God for we were not at the beginning when he created the heavens and the earth nor were we alive during the time that Jesus was on the earth in human flesh. It is through the word that we come into awareness of him and in believing what he says in his word, our faith is born.

Chapter 15 of Romans also tells us that our hope is anchored in the word of God. And we know that hope is what keeps us going in the face of uncertainty, tragedy and disappointments. It is a very important part of the human wellbeing. Our knowledge of the word keeps us going because it provides us with the hope we need. Chapter 15 of 1Corinthians tells us that if our hope was in this life, we would be very miserable. Thanks be to God for his words which is our comfort, instruction, direction, correction and authority.

David in the Psalms testified about the importance of the word of God. He said they were hidden in his heart so that he would not sin against God. He spoke about the delight he found in the word by referring to the word of God as something sweet to his taste, even sweeter than honey to his mouth. He also declared that the word of God gave light to him, that is, understanding and direction in his own journey.

Psalm 119 gives a very good summary of David's appetite for the word of God and in reading this Psalm, we are able to understand how David's transformation came about. He had sinned against God in committing adultery and murder but acknowledged his sins, repented of them and asked God to forgive him and restore him.

It is not clear if David had this awareness of the importance of the word of God before he sinned, but as he outlined in Psalm 119, he had certainly come to that realization.

Now, God's word is his primary means of communicating with us. Think of any one thing that you have come to know about God and you will find that it can be traced back to the Bible.

My own knowledge of God has come to me through the scriptures and I have often shared with others that I have discovered that the answer to every question about life is to be found in the Bible.

However, the usefulness of the word can only be of benefit to us if we have knowledge of it. It matters not how many answers are in the Bible if we do not know how to access it. The people of God are admonished to know the word. Chapter 2 of 2Timothy says that we should study the word of God so that we will be able to discern or distinguish the truth of God.

How then does the idea of having an "appetite for the word of God" applies to us? Appetite is defined as an instinctive desire for food or drink. That is, the desire for food or drink is spontaneous and unthinking. Our appetite is intrinsic – it is a part of us.

The word of God is the only means of our survival and sustenance on the journey. Jesus told the devil that man should not live by bread alone, but by every word which proceeds out of the mouth of God. Bread provides us with sustenance in the physical and the word of God provides us with spiritual sustenance.

There is a spiritual appetite which each of us must have. We must develop it, that is, stimulate our desire for the word of God. Just as in the natural, when our appetite for something is nonexistent, we can also find ourselves in the spiritual, not having an appetite for the word of God. And just as it is detrimental for us to not have an appetite for food and drink, so it is if we do not have one for the word of God.

Jesus has ably demonstrated to us three essential things about living by the word of God:

(1) **The word of God is vital to us**, that is, indispensable to our survival or continuing effectiveness in our Christian living. Jesus was very clear in making the point that while bread was necessary to our physical survival, our flesh would one day perish anyway and what was more vital to us, was the word of God which gives life.

The first chapter of John described Jesus as the word and that he, the word, was God. The word was made flesh and dwelt among us and was the light of the world for Jesus shone into our darkness of sin and by his death, burial and resurrection, has brought us into his marvelous light to be lights ourselves.

Having the word of God in us is having Jesus in us. He is vital to both our physical and spiritual survival. Blessed be our God!

(2) **The word of God is essential to us**, that is, it is of the highest importance in our lives and the means by which we are guided, empowered and equipped to make it into the Kingdom of Heaven. Knowledge of the word of God is very empowering.

It is said that knowledge is power and this is so true for the people of God, for it makes our faith unshakeable and our hope untouchable. The song using words from the Bible says, "For I know whom I have believed; and I'm persuaded that he is able; to keep that which I have committed; unto him against that day…"

The word of God is essential to keeping us energized and enthused about our salvation and the Kingdom of God on our journey there.

(3) **The word of God is critical to us**, that is, it is pivotal or crucial to our future. Jesus, who is the word, says that if his word abide in us we will bring forth fruit and are able to ask of the Father. But if we do not allow his word to abide in us, we will be treated as a dead branch of a tree which is only fit for the fire.

The word of God in us, gives us life and ensures a bright future for us: "And this is life eternal, that they might know thee the only true God, and Jesus Christ, whom thou has sent." "And when the Gentiles heard this, they were glad, and glorified the word of the Lord: and as many as were ordained to eternal life believed."

I know, as an experienced mother, that some children do not like reading. They simply do not have an appetite for it. I know this because that was one of my challenges in raising my daughter. Of course, it could not be ignored because reading was so crucial to her education.

I would repeat to her over and over again that whatever her career ambitions were, she would not be able to achieve them without developing an appetite for reading. I would emphasize that reading was the means by which one's comprehension skill is developed and that her comprehension skill was a necessity for every subject area of her study. For example, understanding a mathematical question was best served by her ability to comprehend what she was being asked to do!

I also know that there are adults who are still challenged in developing an affinity for reading, and when it concerns the Bible, it is even a bigger challenge. Today, technology allows us to hear the reading of the Bible without having to do so ourselves. I encourage us to use whatever media best suitable to us to know the word of God. It is vital; it is essential; it is critical that we do.

The word of God is our life source.

Chapter Four:

THE IMPORTANCE OF THE HOLY SPIRIT

"Except a man be born of water and of the spirit...."

"In the beginning was the Word, and the Word was with God, and the Word was God" are words with special significance to us as believers. Chapter One of the Book of John gives an excellent account of the Word and provides the means by which I am able to lay the foundation of authority for the thoughts I am about to share with you on the Holy Spirit.

The Word being in the beginning; was with God; and was God; is a description of Jesus, for Chapter One went on to say that "... the word was made flesh and dwelt among us ..." We know that Jesus took on the robe of flesh in order to bring about man's redemption and that John was the forerunner to Jesus.

John declared Jesus' coming and when Jesus turned up at the river Jordan to be baptized by him, "he cried, saying, this was he of whom I spake, He that cometh after me is preferred before me: for he was before me."

John clearly identified Jesus as the "Word of God" and repeated that Jesus was before him even though Jesus was born after him in the flesh.

We believing that Jesus is the word, means that every word of Jesus is authentic as the word of God. Why is this point so important?

Because it is Jesus himself who emphasized the importance of the Holy Spirit.

What is your knowledge of the Holy Spirit? And what do you believe about the Holy Spirit? It is so much more than just speaking in tongues! What does Jesus, who is the word of God, has to say about him?

Well, Jesus explained to Nicodemus that every recipient of God's salvation must experience two spiritual rebirth: baptism by water and baptism by fire.

Now, while there is agreement about the rebirth of baptism by water, most of us differ in our understanding and belief about the baptism by fire, that is, the baptism of the Holy Spirit.

Let me share with you my thoughts on the importance of the Holy Spirit according to the word of God:

My first thought is that the Holy Spirit is a deposit that God has made into our lives and you are obligated to manage this deposit to ensure that God gets his fair or agreed return on his deposit. Deposit in this context also means that God has given his Holy Spirit to us as a down payment towards what is yet to come, that is, this same Holy Spirit will be the means by which we are resurrected to receive our inheritance of eternal life at Jesus' second coming.

Verses thirteen and fourteen of Ephesian Chapter One,

"Having believed, you were marked in him with a seal, the promised Holy Spirit, who is a deposit guaranteeing our inheritance until the redemption of those who are God's possession to the praise of his glory."

My second thought is that the Holy Spirit's interactive function in our lives is manifested or evidenced on two levels. These are:

- <u>The Gestative Manifestation</u> in which the interactive function of the Holy Spirit is to draw you to repentance by the conviction of sin; confession of Jesus as Christ; and submission to baptism by water. This is confirmed in verse forty-four of John Chapter Six.

This is best illustrated by the experience of a woman who is pregnant. She is not able to hold the child in her arms while it is in the womb; she can only verbally communicate one way with the child; and any touching of her child takes place with the wall of her womb between them.

Now, no one can deny that she has her child, for while the child is in her womb, she is providing nourishment and stimulation and her interaction with the child is undeniable, especially when there is visible movement of the foetus.

This time spent in the woman's womb is called the "gestation stage" – the child cannot be seen in the physical, yet every evidence of its presence is there as the mother awaits the birth of her child.

So it is with the Holy Spirit. Every believer goes through the gestation stage where the Holy Spirit is at work in our lives to complete the "first works" of repentance, confession and baptism.

- <u>The Birth Manifestation</u> in which the Holy Spirit birth has taken place and you are now empowered with the gifts of the Holy Spirit and spiritual growth is taking place. This is confirmed in verse five of John Chapter Three.

Continuing to use the example of the mother and her child, the first stage of her interaction with her child is pre-birth. When the child is born the interaction can now take place on every level for the rest of their lives.

The mother's communication is now direct; she can see and touch her child at will; and she understands, very well, that after birth, her child must grow and develop into an adult.

Jesus told Nicodemus that he must experience both the birth by water and by fire, so that, as in the case of the mother and her child, we must move from the first birth by water to the second birth by fire.

The process of the first birth, by water, represent the gestation stage of the Holy Spirit. The process of the second birth, by fire, represent the Holy Spirit birthing us into spiritual growth. Just as the child is not expected to stay in the womb indefinitely or remain as a baby at its birth, so are we also not expected to stay in our spiritual gestative stage or remain as spiritual babies. The word of God in the second verse of First Peter Chapter Two, acknowledges us as "newborn babes", and admonishes us to desire the sincere milk of the word that we may grow thereby.

The child who is not growing nor showing certain signs of development, becomes the concern of the parents and the appropriate intervention is sought in the child's behalf. As children of God who must experience spiritual growth and show signs of spiritual development, we are empowered to do so through the birth of the Holy Spirit in us.

This function of the Holy Spirit in our lives ensures our spiritual growth and development. It is unacceptable for us, as God's children to remain as spiritual babies. Verses twelve to fourteen of Hebrews Chapter Five explains: "For when for the time ye ought to be teachers, ye have need that one teach you again which be the first principles of the oracles of God; and are become such as have need of milk, and not of strong meat. For every one that useth milk is unskilful in the word of righteousness: for he is a babe. But strong meat belongeth to them that are of full age, even those who by reason of use have their senses exercised to discern both good and evil."

The Holy Spirit is, therefore, the means by which spiritual nourishment is provided for us throughout our gestation stage, our birth and our growth and development in Christ Jesus.

The third thought to be shared is that the Holy Spirit is the vehicle through which we qualify for the Kingdom of God. To follow on the first two thoughts I have shared so far on the Holy Spirit, we must also understand that the whole idea of God depositing the Holy Spirit into us is to an end, that is, to empower and enable us to qualify for the Kingdom of God.

The Holy Spirit, provides us with nourishment through our different stages of spiritual life, so that, having now been born of the spirit, there are now distinct signs of development which will be indications of whether or not we are qualifying ourselves for the Kingdom of God.

For this purpose, the word of God provides us with three clear goals which we must attain to:

> **<u>1. Spiritual Fruit</u>** of love, joy, peace, longsuffering, gentleness, goodness, faith, meekness and temperance as presented to us in

verses twenty-two and twenty-three of Galatians Chapter Five. Bearing spiritual fruit is the individual indication of growth and development taking place in our lives.

These parts of the spiritual fruit together make us wholesome and tasteful to each other and even more important, to our God through Christ Jesus.

2. Spiritual gifts of the word of wisdom; word of knowledge; faith; healing; miracles; prophecy; discerning of spirits; tongues; and interpretation of tongues as described in First Corinthians Chapter Twelve.

Spiritual gifts which have been deposited in us are not for our benefit only but more so for the corporate benefit of the Household of Faith and the advancement of the Gospel of Jesus Christ.

First Corinthians Chapter Twelve explains to us the functions of these gifts and how they fulfil the corporate objectives God has set for the church, the body of Christ. Note carefully how this chapter explains the central role we play in God's objective and how our spiritual growth is demonstrated through our dedication to fulfilling our purpose.

3. Spiritual Discipline which is demonstrated through the transformation which is continuously taking place in our lives. No one can develop into a disciplined person without first exercising themselves in the principles which will cement, reinforce and maintain that discipline.

What, then, are the principles to which I refer? Knowing the **word of God** is one of them for sure. Jesus, who is the Word of God says that we should not live by bread alone, but by every word which proceed out of the mouth of God.

Think of the purpose for eating bread! We eat to physically sustain ourselves and so we are encouraged to "eat" the word of God that we might be spiritually sustained by the word.

Verses sixteen and seventeen of Second Timothy Chapter Three describes perfectly the purpose of the word of God in our spiritual development: "All scripture is given by inspiration of

God, and is profitable for doctrine, for reproof, for correction, for instruction in righteousness: That the man of God may be perfect, thoroughly furnished unto all good works."

Another principle in which we should exercise ourselves is **fasting**. Fasting? Oh yes! I know it is a challenge for us but it is an absolute necessity for our spiritual development. Jesus taught us that some of the things that need to be purged out of us cannot be done except through fasting and prayer. Fasting as a discipline in our lives is one of most effective way of staying the Christian Course.

Jesus started his assignment with forty days of fasting; faced immediate temptations from Satan where he was tested in the word and overcame Satan through the word. Moses and Elijah did the same – they also fasted forty days before embarking on major assignments given to them by God.

Moses was in the mount for forty days while God delivered to him the Ten Commandments. His assignment to lead God's people into the promise land was not going to be an easy one so God fortified him and strengthened him for the part he would play in God's plan for his people.

Elijah's forty days of fasting was God's way of preparing him for what he would be assigned to do. He was not told before what that assignment would be but in verse sixteen of First Kings Chapter Nineteen, we see that it was to anoint Jehu to be King instead of King Ahab's descendants and to groom Elisha as his replacement. The first assignment was a very dangerous one because of his history with the House of Ahab and the second was to be given the task of grooming someone to replace him indicating that his end was imminent.

Now, we may not be called upon by God to fast for forty days, but we are certainly called upon to make fasting a discipline in our lives. Fasting helps us to purge out the "old leaven" and make room for the Holy Spirit to work in us.

The third principle to exercise ourselves in, is **praying**. It is the lifeline of the believer. It is the line of communication without which no believer can survive. We also make and maintain connection with Heaven through prayer.

Through prayer, we are able to confidently express ourselves to our Heavenly Father and to Jesus our Lord and Savior – to call on Heaven in times of need; ask for our daily bread; seek forgiveness for our failures; be revived and strengthened when we feel weak or we are discouraged; and move Heaven to act at our request.

A wonderful example of this point, is the word of God which says that what is bound or loosed in earth by us is endorsed and accomplished in Heaven.

Jesus is our best example of a life lived with prayer as a discipline. He often went away to pray and was ministered to by the angels. Prayer was Jesus' way of staying on course with his divine assignment.

Our own assignment of advancing the Kingdom of Heaven is no less important and cannot be completed effectively if we fail to develop spiritually through a disciplined life that includes praying often. Hallelujah!!!

My fourth thought on the importance of the Holy Spirit is that he operates as the Power Generator that trips in when we trip out. The Holy Spirit is ever present to continue when we cannot; to speak in our behalf, when we are powerless to speak.

Have you ever had the experience of praying and when words fail you, the Holy Spirit takes over and utter the words to heaven in your behalf? It is an awesome experience.

A power generator is an essential equipment in households that are vulnerable to natural disasters which disrupt their power supply.

Each year, countries on the Atlantic and Pacific coasts as well as in the Caribbean, face the threat of hurricanes and although not every households can afford this commodity, its importance is not dimmed by its absence.

It means, therefore, that those who have this equipment are able to enjoy electricity powered through their generators while those who do not are in darkness or are limited to candles and lamps.

So it is with the Holy Spirit which is the enabling power of God in us. In Chapter One of Acts, Jesus in his last talk with the disciples told them that they would receive power after the Holy Spirit came upon them, enabling and empowering them to be witnesses to the world.

We know from the scriptures and believe by faith that this is true; that these disciples and many others suffered great tribulation and persecution because of the Gospel.

I share this additional thought with you that I believe it was impossible for all of them; every one of them; by themselves, to have borne and overcome such afflictions; such loss; and even choose death, so that they might earn a crown of life eternal I believe that the Holy Spirit was the source of their strength. I believe that it was at work in them, powering them up with divine energy to stay committed to the cause of Christ even unto death. Hallelujah!!!

This function of the Holy Spirit is clearly promised in verse eleven of Mark Chapter Thirteen; verses twenty-six and twenty-seven of Romans Chapter Eight; and verses twenty-eight through thirty-one of Isaiah Chapter Forty in which we are assured that if, or when, we find ourselves in similar situations, we will be able to rely on the power of the Holy Spirit in us to endure our tests.

David spoke, with confidence, that though he walked in the "valley of the shadow of death," he would fear no evil because the presence of God (the Holy Spirit) was with him to comfort him. Jesus also promised us that he would be with us always, that is, he would send the Holy Spirit to us, as an indication of his presence with us.

Another scripture speaks of our ability to do all things through Christ, our strength.

<u>My fifth and final thought</u> on the importance of the Holy Spirit is that He makes a distinction between "Chicken" Christians and "Eagle Christians. I can just imagine how some of you may have raised an eyebrow or two at this point and I am laughing at the thought. But think on it for a moment or two. What do you know about chickens in contrast to what you know about eagles?

Let us consider the chicken! Do you know that the original purpose of the chicken was to be a jungle fowl roaming free, but it was tamed and domesticated to provide food (eggs) and to be food (poultry). The chicken is provided with food; it is provided with a cage; it eats what is determined by someone else and when that person decides to feed it.

Even in our social interactions and communication, a chicken's personality is negative. We refer to persons who exhibit timidity or fear as "chicken." If a man is dominated by his wife and fails to exercise any authority in his household, we refer to him as "henpecked." Even in the context of our sexual conduct, a man who displays affection towards too many women, will, in some cultures, be referred to as a "Rooster."

Let us consider the eagle in contrast to the chicken. Just these few simple facts on the eagle will provide you with a clear vision of the differences between them:

- a) The chicken cannot fly while the eagle, on the other hand, controls the air.
- b) The chicken turns it head to see while the eagle has a clear 360⁰ vision.
- c) The chicken eats just about anything while the eagle eats live meat only which it hunts for itself.
- d) The rooster mates with more than one hen while the eagle is monogamous in that it mates with the same partner each time.
- e) The chicken will use any nest it is given while the eagles use the same nest each year and puts it in an inaccessible place.

Is it not simply wonderful how nature helps us to understand the spiritual things of God? Are you now able to see the simple truth about how it is important that we be not "Chicken Christians", but we should be always striving to become "Eagle Christians?"

Still, I do not want you to forget that virtue is found in the chicken, too, for the word of God refers to the "hen gathering her chickens under her wings" just as He God wants to do with us. The essential point is that a Chicken Christian is still a Christian, but its character, personality and behavior indicate that spiritual development is not taking place at all, or not at the pace indicated by the word of God.

Do you remember the scripture above which referred to those Christians who, when they should be teachers, they had to have someone teach them? Well, when the chickens should be flying, they are still on the ground; when they should be making their own nests and finding their own food, someone is doing it for them.

This sounds like the condition of a baby, for it is unable, at first, to help itself. Only, this is not expected to be a lifelong condition for the infant. It is expected to grow and develop into an independent adult.

So, it is with us as we develop spiritually. We are expected to move from a chicken mentality, character, personality and behavior to "an awesome bird in the sky." Do you know that the eagle represents freedom; majesty; magnificence; and that its mentality, character, personality and behavior is very inspiring to all?

We have every reason to praise and bless the name of our Lord for the Holy Spirit who works within us to bring us to God's perfection. Jesus says, "For without me ye can do nothing." David declared that God would perfect that which concerned him.

Yes, my beloved sojourners, the Holy Spirit is absolutely important to us individually, and as the corporate body of Christ. We are all members of the same body, and if any part is not functioning, it impacts the whole body. It is essential that we are all striving to reach the spiritual goals which God has set for us and equally essential that we understand that anything less will cause us to not inherit the Kingdom of God.

It is, therefore, not just our responsibility for ourselves that is at stake, but our responsibility for each other also.

Chapter Five:

SPRITUAL MATURITY

"But grow in grace, and in the knowledge of our Lord and Saviour Jesus Christ."

The second chapter of this book addressed our spiritual birth and the fact that we start our Christian lives as spiritual infants. What this chapter will present to you are my thoughts that understanding our spiritual infant stage, is as important as understanding that we must obtain spiritual maturity.

In its broadest sense, we understand maturity as fully grown or developed in body and mind; showing the characteristics of mental and physical development; or reaching a desired final condition (for example: a ripe fruit; a mature wine or cheese).

Now there are three points of focus in this definition of maturity albeit I am speaking about maturity in the spiritual context of our lives. They are:

    (1)   **Visible Growth** as in the outward observable changes that everyone who come into contact with us, especially those who knew us before we accepted the Lord Jesus Christ, can see.

            When Jesus entered the temple on the Sabbath day to read, the people of his community were awed at the authority with which he spoke. Jesus grew up before them as the son of a carpenter but now he is impacting them in a new way that "stopped them in their tracks." They asked if this was not the carpenter's son with wonder and disbelief for what they saw and heard was new to them and it also had a tremendous impact on them.

In our physical world we expect every baby to grow from infancy to become a toddler; preschooler; gradeschooler; teenager; and finally, an adult. Of course, each stage comes with visible indications that that child is maturing to the next stage. It is important that the child's transition from one stage to the next is taking place when and how it should be.

So, it is with our spiritual lives. We should be spiritually blossoming; improving; flourishing; thriving; evolving; aging and coming of age; coming into perfection; and becoming seasoned. All these are observable indications of our growth and development in the Lord.

The Book of Ephesians Four explains to us the visible side of spiritual maturity in the individual and how it serves the body of Christ, referring to positions of pastors, teachers, prophets, evangelists and apostles as God's means by which he perfects his church and edifies the body of Christ. By this means, God is bringing his people into perfection and unity so that they will "henceforth be **no more children**, tossed to and fro, and carried about with every wind of doctrine, by the sleight of men, and cunning craftiness, whereby they lie in wait to deceive; but speaking the truth in love, **may grow up into him in all things**, which is the head, even Christ."

(2) **Mental and Psychological** indications of spiritual maturity. The Apostle Paul went on to speak about being "**renewed in the spirit of our minds**" in the same chapter of Ephesians Four. The Apostle Peter admonishes that we "**gird up the loins of our minds**" in the First Book of Peter Chapter One.

In fact, the Apostle Peter presents us with one of the best examples of this point which I am making.

Do you remember how he denied Jesus three times when he came under pressure to identify whether he was a disciple of Jesus or not? Well, it is this same Peter who found himself being questioned once again, this time, by the Jewish authorities after he had healed the man at the Gate Beautiful.

In my view, the clearest indications of Peter's mental and psychological maturity are that he was now able to withstand the intimidation he was experiencing from the Jewish authorities. He declared the Lord Jesus with much boldness and rejoiced when he was whipped and released with threats against his person if ever, he continued to promulgate the gospel of Jesus Christ.

Bear in mind that Peter was now able to do this after he had received power from the Holy Spirit, just as Jesus had promised. The Holy Spirit is therefore the key to our spiritual maturity.

(3) **Purpose Served** by maturity. In other words, maturity should take place to what end? Why do parents ensure that their children are growing and maturing into adults?

What is expected of these children when they attain adult status?

In the ideal situation, every child who becomes an adult is expected to assume responsibility for themselves. They are also expected to establish their independence; become law-abiding citizens; become parents themselves and make appropriate contributions to their community.

So also, the Christian is expected to mature into a believer who is thoroughly furnished in the word of God; living victoriously over sin and temptations; practicing discipleship; acquiring the fruit of the spirit and the gifts of God for the perfection and edification of the body of Christ.

So far, we understand that spiritual maturity is the final stage of the Christian's birth, growth and development. Each stage has its own imperative as indicated by the word of God. It was Jesus who told Nicodemus that Spiritual Birth was an imperative when he told him that he MUST be born again. The Apostles themselves emphasized to the churches of their day that Spiritual Growth (verses one and two of First Peter Chapter Two) was an imperative as well as Spiritual Maturity (verses five to eight of Second Peter Chapter One and verses six to eight of Colossians Chapter Two).

And finally, let me share with you my thoughts on what are some of the indications that we are attaining spiritual maturity:

(1) We have developed a quiet confidence in the word of God. Meditate on verses seven to fourteen of Second Timothy Chapter One.

(2) We are not shaken in the face of challenges or adverse situations. Consider the Shunamite Woman in Second Kings Chapter Four; Job in the Book of Job Chapter One; and the three Hebrews Boys in Daniel Chapter There.

(3) We have developed the ability to see God and not ourselves. That is, we realize that this whole business of salvation is not about us, but about what God is doing; and being willing to let God have his way. Read verses one to ten of Second Corinthians Twelve in which Paul declares his willingness to "take pleasure in infirmities, in reproaches, in necessities, in persecutions, in distresses for Christ's sake."

(4) We are "patiently waiting" on God. Many of us do wait on God, but with impatience, murmurings and anxiety. Verse seven of Psalm Thirty-seven says "Rest in the Lord, and wait patiently for him…."

(5) We are experiencing God in an intimate way. That is, we have reached a place in our relationship with God where we are no longer motivated by a sense of duty or obligation. It is now our absolute delight just to be with

him. David declares that his desire for the Lord was as driven as "a hart seeking after water."

(6) We have developed the spiritual discipline of prayer; fasting and knowing the word of God. We must apply ourselves to these principles in order to maintain the highest standards of righteousness. Jesus taught these principles as recorded in verse twenty-nine of Mark Chapter Nine.

(7) We are able to maintain a standard of holiness out of sight of others. That is, when we are out of the spotlight or the presence of other believers, we are still able to do what is right. David declared that he would walk within his house with a perfect heart.

When we are in our house, we are in our private space where we will sometimes behave at our worst. However, out of the sight of man is not out of the sight of God.

Maturity means maintaining a consistent standard of holiness.

Chapter Six:

STRIVING FOR THE "ELECTUS"

"Wherefore the rather, brethren, give diligence to make your calling and election sure."

Every year, in America, the world of professional sports engage in a drafting system. This is a method of allocating players to various professional teams. It operates with the objective of keeping the competition among teams balanced, so that no one team or teams can manipulate the system to an unfair advantage.

The areas of professional sports most familiar to us are basketball, football and baseball. These are multimillion and even billion-dollar industries in which professional players are paid millions of dollars to participate.

Now, while there are rules which govern how teams behave and how members of those teams behave, the onus of each team's success rests on the ability, integrity and performance of each team member. The greatness of the team is the collective greatness of each team member, and these professional sports provide individuals who aspire to be great and/or rich with opportunities to do so. However, there is a path which they must take to get there.

The journey to playing professional sports usually starts at high school; then college, if you are great at it; and finally, on to playing professionally in the major leagues. Every athlete who aspires to reach the pinnacle of a career in sports knows that their very best is the least they can contribute towards their goals. When they perform at the high school level, they are giving their coaches an opportunity to see their potential as well as their abilities and natural talent to make it to the top.

Coaches, who must choose these teams to represent the schools, have a limited number of positions on these teams. They are therefore hard pressed to ensure that the very best of those that are available to them, make it to their teams. Some coaches will even travel outside of their schools to recruit talented players from other schools in an effort to ensure the success of their teams.

How then do players who are ambitious of being on that team, ensure that they are chosen? There are many players who have the same talent, but not everyone will make it on to the teams. What can they do to separate themselves from the other players and ensure that they get selected? What kind of preparation of themselves is required to make them stand out among their peers? What is the kind of support they need from others to become successful?

As I share my thoughts on this topic with you, I am doing so by answering the above questions and highlighting the components to succeeding in "making our calling and election to the Kingdom of God sure."

(1) No one can become a member of a sports team without meeting the basic requirements of knowing how to play the game and what the rules of the game are. At this stage, opportunities to be considered for the team are open to everyone. They are all playing under the watchful eyes of the coaches and are being evaluated in all the areas that will determine a player's suitability.

(2) Players who are ambitious of being selected know that they must impress the coaches with a consistent standard of play as well as show that they are improving with each opportunity that is given to them.

The most important point to be made here, is the fact that the natural talent, skill and potential of the player cannot, by itself, guarantee these players a place on the team. It must be accompanied by the character traits of integrity; discipline; undivided commitment; and team spirit. These characteristics are critical to the success of any team and these coaches are going to see to it that each player is a well-rounded member of his team by ensuring that the academic performance of each player meets the schools' evaluation standards as well.

(3) This is what separates the players: there are many very talented players who exhibit no discipline, integrity or moral conduct which cannot be overlooked in their consideration for the teams. Others have such poor academic outcomes, that no amount of talent and skill can compensate for that.

Therefore, the player who wishes to stand out must aim to achieve all these objectives and display consistency in doing so.

(4) Support from others is critical to the motivation of the players whether this support comes from family members, friends; coaches; or well-wishers. It is one of our social needs that we be acknowledged or recognized when we do well. Our successes are empty if we do not have anyone to share them with.

I recall an occasion in high school when, as an athlete, I was slated to run against another competitor from a school at which I used to be a student. All the students from that school who knew me, were taunting me that I would be beaten in the race. As I waited for the starter, my coach came by and whispered in my ear, "You can beat her in this race." I don't know where I found it in me, but I got out of the starting blocks and never looked back until that race was finished. Of course, she came in behind me!

Now, I have used these relatable points about the world of sports to bring across to you the whole concept of "making your calling and election sure."

The gospel of Jesus Christ is preached to all of us and we can all respond positively, though we do not. Those of us who do, when we have fulfilled the basic requirements of salvation: repentance; confession; and baptism; we have entered into a spiritual assembly of saints called the "Ecclasias."

This word is used over one hundred times in the New Testament's original language and is interpreted as "the called out." Today's bible translations replaced it with the word "church" but when Jesus spoke to Peter after his resurrection, he told him that "upon this rock I will build my ecclasias." Jesus was in effect, telling Peter that those who accepted the gospel would become a part of the "called out people" of God.

So what is the key point in the Apostle's exhortation to us to make both our "calling" and our "election" sure? Let us return to the point of the ambitious player who wants to make the team and actually does so. Does his place on the team guarantees him a place in every game? Certainly not! That is entirely up to his performance as a team member! He has to ensure that his game is consistently good and that the team's success while it may be attributed to all its members, he is singled out as a major contributor to that success.

A basketball player cannot singly win a game but the records can indicate whether his level of play in that game is the main reason for the team's victory. If he wants to be always "selected" to play, he has to maintain a consistently high standard of play.

It is the same principle for us: as the players make the team and are required to perform at a standard that ensure their inclusion in each game, so as Christians we have become members of the "called out by God" also known as the "Ecclasias," and must now ensure that we are selected for the Kingdom of God.

The word associated with being the "select" or the "elect" of God is known as the "Electus." This is a declaration of Jesus who said in Matthew Chapter Twenty-two and the fourteenth verse, "for many are called, but few are chosen." It is the basis for the Apostle's exhortation that we do not settle for a place in the "called out" (the "ecclasias") but that we diligently seek to be among the "elected" (the "electus").

As I draw on the parallel of dedicated athletes who must tune their bodies and minds for what they hope to accomplish; and make the necessary sacrifices to achieve their goals, so I encourage us to "gird up the loins of our minds;" exercise ourselves in righteousness (right speaking; right doing; right thinking and right attitude); and develop the determination modelled by Paul who said in Romans Chapter Eight, verses thirty-seven to thirty-nine, "…..in all these things we are more than conquerors through him that loved us. For I am persuaded, that neither death, nor life, nor angels, nor principalities, nor powers, nor things present, nor things to come, nor height, nor depth, nor any other creature, shall be able to separate us from the love of God, which is in Christ Jesus our Lord."

In my own words, I have often declared that "neither demons, nor men, nor whatever it be," will be able to stop me from attaining the Crown of Life which the righteous Judge shall give me according to my works (for faith without works is pointless). I am running my race with patience, looking unto Jesus, the author and finisher of my faith. I am determine and determined to be in the "'electus." May our God of Grace and his son Jesus Christ see all of us through in this endeavour.

Chapter Seven:

KNOWING AND BELIEVING WHO YOU ARE

"But you are a chosen generation, a royal priesthood, an holy nation….."

As we consider the topic of this Chapter about knowing and believing who we are, an appropriate question, at this juncture, would be how do we establish our identity, and why having an identity is important.

Well, in the simplest of language and definition, identity is like an individual label which is given to us. When we are about to purchase a product in the marketplace, we are presented with a label and description of the product; details of what it contains; and the quantity of its contents. This information is used to easily identify what we are purchasing and over time we begin to trust and expect that what we read on the outside will be what we actually find in our use of the product.

Our own identity is established in a similar way with more elements to it. At birth, our labeling consist of our nationality; gender; family heritage; physical attributes; cultural heritage; and our name. This is our basic identity, for as we grow older, it widens to include our profession; beliefs; politics; marriage; children; employment; talents; philosophy; and successes as well as failures.

Our identity says who we are and that is how we are known to others. It is also the information which we have of ourselves. For example, whose daughter or son are we? What is our nationality? To which family do we belong? In essence, our knowledge of ourselves is how we answer our questions about who we are.

Now, one cannot talk about identity without the mention of self-esteem, for it plays a very important function in how we feel, how we behave, and how we value ourselves. Self-esteem is simply the esteem in which we hold ourselves. It is influenced by the information we have about ourselves; our behavior; our experiences; and how we are viewed by others, that is, how others evaluate and value us.

While Jesus and his disciples were visiting a town called Caesarea Philippi, he asked them two very important questions about himself. The first was: "Whom do men say that I the Son of man am?" From the scriptures of Matthew Chapter Sixteen and Mark Chapter Eight, we see that several answers were given to him by his disciples.

They reported to Jesus that some thought that he was John the Baptist; others thought that he was Elias, Jeremias or one of the other prophets.

Jesus' second question to them was: "But whom say ye that I am?" Simon Peter, in answering, "Thou are the Christ, the Son of the living God," received a delightful response from Jesus that it was his Father in Heaven who had revealed who Jesus was to him. Jesus went on to tell Peter what his future would be like; about the rewards of heaven which he would receive; and the power that he would have to bind and loose anything upon the earth and have it sanctioned in heaven. Awesome!

My take away thoughts from these questions of Jesus to his disciples, is the importance of a person's identity. Just let your imagination embrace the religious context of the time in which Jesus was carrying out his mission of mankind's redemption. Think for a moment how dangerous it would be for anyone, in those days, to declare himself as the Son of God or to tell a religious group of people that when they see him, they are actually seeing God, for he and God are one. Did you note from the reading of Matthew Chapter Sixteen, how Jesus told them to keep the information about who he was, a secret, until he was ready to declare it?

I believe that the wisdom which Jesus exercised, in timing the identification of himself, is not to be confused with fear. Jesus knew who he was; knew what he was about; and had no identity conflicts about himself. He was told on numerous occasions that he could not be the Christ for they knew him from his childhood as the son of a carpenter; they knew his family members; and were in fact very offended by him. They even threatened to hurt him on more than one occasion. Others, such as the religious authorities refused to believe or accept him as who he claimed himself to be. They went as far as to tell him that he was Satan and that he was a liar.

This is a very important point to be emphasized because Peter, after such a profound revelation of who Jesus was, did experience a crisis of identity when he was asked, later on, if he was one of the disciples at the trial of Jesus. In fact, Jesus told Peter that it would happen before it did and, every word of God being true, Peter experienced a serious crisis in identity "before the cock crow."

While Jesus timed the revelation of who he was out of wisdom, the same cannot be said of Peter who was motivated by fear.

He was afterward ashamed of himself and repented of his failure to identify himself with Jesus. But to Peter's credit, and a perfect example for us who are struggling with our own identity crisis as Christians, he quickly recovered; joined the other disciples to comfort each other while they waited to see the fulfilment of the resurrection of Jesus.

Note how after his resurrection, Jesus reinforced Peter in John Chapter Twenty-one by asking him three times if he loved him and so established for Peter a new identity which was no longer limited to that of a fisherman, but now appointed by Jesus to "feed his sheep" and "follow him." And note also, how Peter, having embraced his new identity, gave a different account of himself when he was challenge by the religious authorities about his faith and his actions in the temple. The Book of Acts Chapter Five gives us the full account of Peter's experience, especially how he boldly identified himself as a witness of Jesus and rejoiced that he was counted worthy to suffer shame for the name of Jesus.

What then do our own identity of being a Christian mean to us? How do we feel about ourselves and how is our behavior and lifestyle impacted by who we are as Christians? What do we know and believe about ourselves as Christians.

My own thoughts and experiences have brought me to a place of quiet confidence in who we are as Christians. I know, based upon the word of God, and believe, by my faith, that we are the people of the true and living God. This is what I know and believe:

(1) We are so loved of God that he sent his only son, Jesus to die in our place.

(2) We are born again according to John Chapter Three through the redemptive blood of Jesus Christ. This birth is not a physical one but rather a spiritual rebirth. Our sins are forgiven so that the penalty of death is no longer over us.

(3) We now have direct access to God through Jesus who gives us this authority in John Chapter Fourteen.

(4) We are now known and are called to behave as sheep; servants; saints; friends; disciples; and sons of God.

(5) We are known of God, Jesus and the angels of heaven and are recognized by Satan and his angels as belonging to God.

(6) We are the chosen people of God, belonging to a royal spiritual priesthood and a holy nation of people called out by him to show that he has called us from darkness into his marvelous light, that is, from ignorance of God into the glorious knowledge of who he is.

(7) Jesus is with us always according to his promise to us in Matthew Chapter Twenty-eight.

(8) Eternal life is our reward if we stay true to God and his word so that our obedience is seen in the way we live, speak, act and even in our attitudes.

In the current context of our lives, it is not only our identity that is important but also who we identify with. Societal approval and esteem is accorded to a person based on who they are as well as who they are associated with. Christians do not any more enjoy society's approval or esteem as before and it is becoming life threatening for some of us who have chosen God's way.

To combat this kind of negative energy towards us and stay true to our calling, purpose and destiny, we have to find strength in the knowledge of who we are and whose we are.

The members of the royal family are very confident about themselves by virtue of their place in society. They are highly esteemed and those who become a member of the royal family by marriage are accorded the level of respect that comes with that new status.

We, the people of the true and living God, should feel confident in who we are even more than they do, because our position is one that is established in heaven by the King above all kings and the Lord above all lords.

The opinion of others cannot change who we are just as the opinion of the people could not change who Jesus was. Not everyone believed or accepted Jesus even though they were witnesses of his miracles and present when he taught.

Do not expect our experiences to be different. Jesus says we should not marvel that the world hates us, for we are not of the world though we are in it.

May the knowledge of who we are be our strength and keeps us dedicated and committed to the cause of God who is depending on us to do his will. He has given us an identity that is above any other.

Not only are we different by our rebirth in Christ Jesus, but we have been "made a little lower than the angels and have been crowned with glory and honor at creation."

Let us all "walk worthy of the Lord unto all pleasing, being fruitful in every good work, and increasing in the knowledge of God."

Paul says, in Romans Chapter One, that he was not ashamed of the gospel of God for it is the power of God unto salvation… There is therefore no shame in who we are!

Chapter Eight:

ENSURING YOUR SOUL IS AT PEACE

"Therefore being justified by faith, we have peace with God through our Lord Jesus Christ...."

What would you answer if you were asked the question: "Which do you prefer, that your mind be at rest, or that your soul be at peace?" It is my endeavor to discuss the difference between them in this chapter so that you can get a sense of how important it is to maintain your peace with God.

Romans Chapter Five tells us that because of sin, we were enemies of God, that is, we were not at peace with God. But Jesus, by his death, and through our faith in him, has reconciled us to God so that we are now justified before God, and able to enjoy a relationship of peace with him.

This chapter will first, provide you with some definitions of our "minds being at rest" versus our "souls being at peace." It will also facilitate your contemplation on the connection between them.

When our "mind is at rest," there is no worry; agitation; stress; discomfort; pressure or tension. It also means that there is no threat to our person (whether it be physical; social; financial; or spiritual); we are relaxed and at ease; and, we are free from anxiety and concern. Let me also emphasize, that it also means that we are not likely to be "found out" or "uncovered" for our actions.

When we speak of our "soul," we are referring to a person's moral or emotional nature, as well as their sense of identity and individuality. The bible refers to both the physical person (as in "fourteen souls" or the "soul that sinneth"), as well as the heart of the person (as in "the soul of Johnathan was knit with the soul of David").

The "soul being at peace" means, therefore, that the person is free from conflict; strife; or condemnation; as well as the person's heart is in harmony; contentment and serenity.

In summarization of these definitions and setting them in their context, when we speak of "our minds being at rest" we are referring to the state of our minds; that is, how we feel after our decisions and actions have been taken. When we speak of our "souls being at peace," it goes beyond the mere state of our minds to involve our standing before God. The mind is about our decisions and actions and our soul is about our standing before God for those decisions and actions which we have taken.

I cannot think of a better example, than King David, to make the topic, "Ensuring your Soul is at Peace," easily understood. Let us start with First Samuel Chapter Twenty-six in which David, who was not yet King, while fleeing for his life from King Saul, hid himself in the wilderness of Ziph.

When it was reported to Saul that David and his men were hid in the wilderness, he came down with three thousand chosen men to kill David who had knowledge of Saul's whereabout because he had the opportunity of observing Saul's movements through his spies.

When Saul and his men settled down to rest, David and one of his men, Abishai, went down into Saul's camp and found him sleeping and all the men who were with him asleep also.

Abishai encouraged David to take the opportunity that he thought God had given him to kill Saul, but David disagreed saying, "Destroy him not: for who can stretch forth his hand against the LORD's anointed, and be guiltless?" David said furthermore, "As the LORD liveth, the LORD shall smite him; or his day shall come to die; or he shall descend into battle, and perish. The LORD forbid that I should stretch forth mine hand against the LORD's anointed: but, I pray thee, take thou now the spear that is at his bolster, and the cruse of water, and let us go."

What David faced, in that moment, was a choice between having his "mind at rest" or his "soul at peace." If he had killed Saul, his mind would have been at rest, because he would not have to run for his life any more. However, he also recognized that in solving his problem by killing Saul, while his mind would have been at rest, his soul would certainly not be at peace.

Note how he reasoned with Abishai that it was impossible for him to go against the will of God in killing someone who was anointed by God. David in this moment chose to be at peace with God rather than to simply put his mind at rest.

Let us now examine this same David, who is now King and who is confronted with the same dilemma of choosing to have his "mind at rest" or his "soul at peace."

One day, while he was taking a break from fighting, he walked upon the roof of his house and observed Bathsheba, the wife of one of his soldiers, Uriah, bathing herself. What King David did after he saw her is detailed in Second Samuel Chapters Eleven and Twelve.

King David committed the act of adultery with Bathsheba and when he found out that she was pregnant, he sent for Uriah and sent him home to be with his wife. However, being an honorable man, he refused to go and be with his wife while his fellow soldiers were away fighting for David.

When David failed to persuade him to go home, he gave him a letter instructing the captain of the army to put him at the front of the battle so that he would be killed. Uriah unknowingly, took his own death warrant to the captain and was killed in the battle.

As soon as David received the report that Uriah was dead, he sent and fetched Bathsheba and married her. You can read for yourself, the lengths to which David went to cover his actions and how, at first, had succeeded in keeping his secret intact, and had all the ends of his problem taken care of.

What David had succeeded in doing this time and the choice he had made on this occasion, was to put his mind at rest. Was his soul at peace with God? Did he have God's approval?

When our actions are not known to others, and we are not exposed for our wrong doings, our minds may be at rest. But it is never at peace with God until we confess and repent of it. We do not escape even when it seems to be so for a while. When we sin, we never have God's approval and what we have done in effect, is put ourselves in direct conflict with him for he is a righteous and holy God.

David was now in jeopardy of his soul. He may have gotten away with it, it would seem, but his standing before God was not a good one. It was clear that he was so content with the outcome of his actions that when God sent Nathan, the prophet, to tell him the story of the poor man and his one sheep, he was willing to kill again not realizing that he was the man, and that his soul was in jeopardy.

Credit to King David is however due, for when he realized that it was all about him and his heinous actions to an innocent man, Uriah, he immediately admitted his guilt and fell before God in repentance. The attitude and demeanor of David is such an example for all of us who have and will find ourselves choosing at times, to have our mind at rest over our souls being at peace with our God.

God, himself, refers to David as a man after his own heart and Psalm Chapter Fifty-one is a model prayer of repentance. David laid it all out before the Lord. He not only confess his sins, but in asking for God's forgiveness, he was putting himself back on track with the objective of restoring the peace he once enjoyed with God.

Would to God, we all strive to make the right choice at all times. The choice to have our minds at rest may not include our souls at peace with God. But, and let me emphasize this, when our souls are at peace with God, our minds are automatically at rest.

We need not fear for our sins are forgiven; we have been set free; and we, now having been justified, have peace with God through our Lord Jesus Christ.

Chapter Nine:

OUR OBLIGATION TO OTHERS

And the Lord said unto Cain, "Where is Abel thy brother?"
And he said, "I know not: Am I my brother's keeper?"

The story of the brothers, Cain and Abel, is the first incident of "accountability for the next person" that is recorded in the bible. This story in the Book of Genesis, about these first brothers to have a conflict, have been a reference point for every kind of relationship whether they be with family members; neighbors or strangers.

Was Cain held accountable for Abel because of what he did to his brother, or was there a deeper principle being established by God when he asked him where his brother was? After all, God already knew where he was and what had happened to him. I believe there was!

Accountability speaks to being answerable for our actions and their outcomes. Accountability for someone else would, therefore mean, being answerable for our actions for and against other persons.

Obligation, on the other hand, speaks to a course of action imposed upon us by society, our laws, or our conscience, by which we are bound or restricted. Obligations, therefore, come with some form of accountability, some examples of which can be found in the following:

(1) Social obligations such as the agreed behaviors imposed by society upon its citizens. These behaviors may also be based on laws as well as the collective conscience of the society. Members of the society set standards for ethics, courtesy, equity, charity, to name a few.

(2) Legal obligations which are rooted in the laws of that society. These laws would automatically have social components to them though it may not be influenced by conscience. A law against theft would have the social component of requiring its citizens to refrain from depriving other citizens of their property, while not necessarily being an issue of conscience or moral.

(3) Obligations which are determined by conscience will vary from person to person because it is an individual decision being made even though its outcome may affect others as well as the society. To explain, if the law against killing is breached by someone whose conscience does not restrict him in this act, the death of the victim affects individuals, families and the society at large.

As Christians, we are uniquely positioned to meet the above social standards of obligation and accountability as members of our individual societies, the spiritual standards of obligation and accountability of our Christian community in Christ Jesus.

Jesus, in response to the question of whether it was right to pay taxes, said that we should "give unto Caesar, the things which are Caesar, and unto God, the things which are God's." That is a clear indication of how God wants us to behave as Christians. We must honor our social obligations to our society as much as we should honor our spiritual obligations to God.

I know that we understand our societal obligations to the other members of our society. There are standards of conduct which have been set by us through our culture, law and personal ethics, and we are obligated to abide by them or suffer the consequences for not doing so. The laws of our society do not just tell us what our restrictions are, but also the penalty for our noncompliance.

We, the people of God, have parallel obligations and accountability to God which includes how we treat each other. There are many scriptures that explain what those obligations are and some of those scriptures also explain the penalty for our noncompliance.

These instructions are presented both in the negative as well as in the positive. Let us start with the story of the two siblings, Cain and Abel.

Genesis Chapter Four gives the account of the two brothers making their presentations to God, and the brother, Cain, having his rejected because God found it to be unacceptable. There is no record of Abel doing anything that would have caused his brother to take his life, except that his presentation was pleasing to God.

Cain's slaying of his brother would appear to be out of hatred, jealousy and envy, all negative feelings with negative outcomes. There is a saying that "the container storing the chemical, is more damaged that the container into which it is poured." In other words, Abel was affected by the "pouring out" of Cain's venom, but Cain was destroying himself by "storing" hatred, jealousy and envy in his heart, and he did suffer the consequence of his action.

This is the first example of what God requires of us concerning each other. The Ten Commandments also sets out our obligations towards God as well as ours towards each other. Note that we are not just restricted from killing, which we all find to be heinous, but we are also restricted from lying on and to each other; stealing from each other; neglecting to obey and honor our parents; betraying our spouses; and, oh yes, envying our neighbors.

I know that the last one is done on the inside, but God restricts us from envying our neighbors of even their possessions.

So that we might have a better understanding of these obligations, let us consider them in the following categories:

Christians:

We are referred to as "light" and "salt" to the world by Jesus and commanded to preach the gospel to others and make disciples of them. He also commanded us to love each other including our enemies.

We have an obligation to live our lives in such a manner that it brings enlightenment to our communities and the world. Our interaction with the world should be of flavor, that is, persons who come in contact with us should be left feeling good about us and our faith.

Paul admonishes us to support each other by "lifting up the hands that hang down and the feeble knees." The Christian walk is not an easy one and we are encouraged to lend our support to each other so that we all can succeed in completing this journey.

Paul also likened us to the members of our bodies. Each member has a role to play, upon which all the other members depend on. The whole body depends upon the eye for sight is only one example.

The thorny issue of forgiveness is another obligation we have towards each other. We owe it to ourselves to forgive, because it is commanded, not so much for the benefit of the offender but for our own benefit. When we forgive we release ourselves from bitterness and hatred and empower ourselves to boldly ask our Father in Heaven for his forgiveness. He says unless we first forgive, we will not be able to receive his forgiveness.

<u>Parents:</u>

As Christian parents, our parental obligations are not only prescribed by our society through our culture and our laws. We have a divine obligation given to us by God, who tells us that we should bring up our children in "the way they should go."

This speaks to an obligation to provide our children with direction in life. This cannot be left entirely to the social aspects of our lives, such as what they are socially, culturally, and educationally exposed to.

We are commanded to teach them about God and direct their lives in alignment with the word of God. When we instruct them, they should know that it is because God requires it of them. When we correct them, they should know it is because God disapproves of that conduct.

They should be made aware from the time that they can understand us, that they are God's children and that we have been assigned as parents to ensure their safety, health and wellbeing. They should always be considered in the context of whose they are, and our own accountability for the role we play or fail to play before God.

They are also given their own instruction by God to love and obey us, hence, there is an additional obligation on our part to ensure that they are taught that, and how important their obligation to do so, is to God. It is the only one of the Ten Commandments that has a promised attached to it.

Finally, our parental authority should not be abused towards our children. God commands that we do not provoke them to wrath. I do believe that "wrath" means, not just anger, but also frustration, humiliation and rebellion.

Pastors:

Every word of God being true, I must include Pastors in particular, and church leadership in general, as a category by itself.

Jesus told Peter to feed his sheep three times. That is how important the roles the Pastor and the leadership of the church play in the life of the believer.

When the scriptures describe both God and Jesus as shepherd, there should be a "fearful" awareness by pastors of the awesome obligation which have been laid on them. "Fearful" in this context should be both the reverent respect for God, as in the fear of the Lord, and fear of the consequence of your failure to take care of God's sheep. Pastors should carry out their obligations to God's sheep with both respect for God and dread of his displeasure.

This is well-supported by the Old Testament in Jeremiah Chapter Twenty-three and Ezekiel Chapter Thirty-four and the New Testament in Matthew Chapter Eighteen, Mark Chapter Nine and Luke Chapter Nineteen.

Paul also cements this in Acts Chapter Twenty and verse Twenty-eight: "Take heed, therefore, unto yourselves, and to all the flock, over the which the Holy Ghost hath made you overseers, to feed the church of God, which he hath purchased **with his own blood.**"

My final thought on the topic is our reward for meeting our obligations to others. Jesus says in Matthew Chapter Twenty-five that when he comes in his glory and all the holy angels with him, he is going to gather all the nations before him and separate them into two groups: the sheep and the goats.

The group which is called the sheep will be welcomed into the Kingdom of God as inheritors and blessed of the Father. They will be told that they fed him when he was hungry; gave him water for his thirst; took him in as a stranger; clothed him when he was naked; visited him when he was sick and went to see him when he was in prison. And when they ask when was that done to him, Jesus says his answer will be, "Inasmuch as ye have done it unto one of the least of these my brethren, ye have done it unto me."

The group which is called the goats will have the opposite experience. They will be rejected by Jesus, who will tell them, "Inasmuch as ye did it not to one of the least of these, ye did it not to me."

The "sheep" will enter into life eternal while the "goats" shall go away into everlasting punishment.

Remember, our labor is not in vain. If we commit to meeting and maintaining our obligations to others, eternal life is promised as our reward.

Chapter Ten:

YOU ARE EMPOWERED TO STAY "ON COURSE."

"I have fought a good fight, I have finished my course, I have kept the faith:"

Throughout my many years in the workplace, one of the most common complaints of workers has been their frustration from being given responsibilities without the requisite authority to carry them out. In other words, workers are given the responsibility to carry out their roles and functions in the workplace, but are not "empowered" to do so.

Empowerment is defined as being given the legal power or official authority to decide and act. An employee who has been given the position of manager cannot be an effective manager without the requisite legal power or official authority to make decisions or take actions.

Another complaint in the workplace is the frequency of changes in policy, direction and goals without a sense of achievement or accomplishment.

The sense of stability that an ambitious worker enjoys in the workplace is one that includes understanding of the vision, mission and values of the organization. The articulated vision, mission and values of the organization clarify the "to what end" (vision); "means by which" (mission); and "principles which will guide decisions and actions" (values).

Every organization is impacted by its ability, or lack of ability, to articulate their vision, mission and values to their employees. When an organization succeeds in doing so, what they are doing, in effect, is laying down a solid foundation on which they can build "buy-in" and commitment from their employees. No house can stand for a long time if its foundation is not well laid.

Any organization that is frequently changing its vision, mission and values risk its credibility and effectiveness. Change is necessary in the monitoring and evaluation process, but, self-defeating if those changes are frequent and lacking in purpose. The organization must, therefore, be able to stay "on course."

When we speak of "on course," in this context, we are referring to the organization going in the right direction and being on the right path.

(1) What I have been able to synthesize from these two complaints of the workplace is that: For an organization to succeed, it must have its goals and objectives articulated in its vision and mission. And of equal importance, is the articulated values of the organization that must include empowerment of the workers.

(2) It is important that the organization stays "on course." That is, the organization through its vision, mission and values, must lay for itself, a solid foundation which will ensure its ongoing success.

This final chapter which I am sharing with you, on our being empowered to stay "on course," is another Christian obligation which I choose to address separately from the penultimate chapter on our obligation to others. This chapter addresses our obligation to the "Cause of God"; how God has articulated his vision, mission and values to us; and that he has empowered us to carry out our obligations in his "Cause."

As Jesus used relatable stories of everyday life to explain to his audience spiritual ideas, so is my attempt in this chapter, by referring you to my experience and understanding of what is a successful organization.

Starting with the word "cause," it is defined as (a) the basis for action or reason for a response; (b) a goal or principle being served with dedication and zeal; and (c) the interests of a person or group in a struggle. In the context of what God is about, let us review Chapter Three and verses Sixteen to Seventeen of the Book of John:

> "For God so loved the world, that he gave his only begotten Son, that whosoever believeth in him should not perish, but have everlasting life. For God sent not his Son into the world to condemn the world; but that the world through him might be saved."

God's Vision for the World

What was God responding to and what was the basis for his action? Romans Chapter Three and verse Twenty-three says, "For all have sinned and come short of the Glory of God." When Adam sinned, we were all counted as sinners. This is the spiritual heritage of Adam.

What Adam's sin did was to put us in jeopardy of death, for Romans Chapter Six and verse Twenty-three tells us that the penalty of sin is death. But "it is not the will of God that any should perish, but that all come to repentance," so "he gave his only begotten Son, that whosoever believeth on him, should not perish, but have everlasting life."

God's vision for the world, is that the world through his Son, Jesus, might be saved. God is responding to our need to be saved from death and be restored into fellowship with him forever.

God's Mission

An organization's mission statement tells of the path it will take to achieving its vision. In the Cause of God, the goal and principle being served is that "all should not perish but come to repentance."

How is this goal being served with dedication and zeal? God's plan of salvation: repentance, confession, baptism and a lifestyle of righteousness, is the path to our redemption. God "sent not his Son into the world to condemn the world, but that the world through him might be saved."

Jesus did not just come to earth to die for us. He also came to show us how to attain to life everlasting by modeling for us each step to be taken on our way back to God.

God's Values

In the Cause of God, what are the interests (that is, right, claim or benefit) of the parties involved in the cause? What are those values which God has established as guiding principles for decisions and actions in his cause?

God's interest in his cause, is that he succeeds in saving us; and our interest in the cause of God, is that we be counted worthy to receive eternal life.

As in the case of the organization, where its values are framed by it rules and regulations, so are God's rules and regulations, the framework for our Christian values. The organizations' values determine its business conduct and the work ethic of its employees. So does God's values for us determine our own conduct.

To continue the parallel being made of the organization, we know that a successful organization is one that empowers its workers to achieve the goals and objectives which are set for them. If one of a manager's responsibilities is to manage the performance of the members of his team, he must be given the requisite legal power and official authority to address non-compliance in performance as much as reward those who perform with excellence.

Jesus, before his death, told his disciples that he would send the Holy Spirit to empower them, in his absence, to continue in their discipleship. After his resurrection, he gave them the commission to go into all the world and preach the gospel: baptizing; teaching and making disciples. At his ascension, he told them that they would receive power after the Holy Spirit came upon them and that they would be empowered to proclaim the gospel of Jesus Christ throughout the world.

Jesus at the time of his departure had completed his assignment of articulating God's vision, mission and values for mankind.

His disciples, and us today, have been recruited into the Cause of God, to help to save the world according to the vision and mission of God.

Having knowledge of our purpose and destiny in God; that we are the "picture" that the world sees; that we are called by God to be the "light" and "salt" of the world, how do we stay on course? How are we empowered to do so?

The Apostle Paul says in Second Corinthians Chapter Four, that "seeing we have this ministry, as we have received mercy, so we faint not." The Apostle Paul, recognizing his call to the ministry of Christ and having received such mercy from God when he was persecuting the people of God, he is empowered to stay on course.

Paul went on to say in verses eight to ten: "We are troubled on every side, yet not distressed; we are perplexed, but not in despair; persecuted, but not forsaken; cast down, but not destroyed; always bearing about in the body the dying of the Lord Jesus, that the life also of Jesus might be made manifest in our body."

Jesus is our best example of staying on course. He understood the Cause of his Father; he dedicated himself to his Father's Cause in his declaration that he came for the sole purpose of doing the will of his Father; laid down his life for the Cause; and prayed to the Father on our behalf that the Father would keep on course.

The Apostle Paul is another example of staying on course. In recounting his experience, he says in Second Corinthians Chapter Eleven,

> "...in labours more abundant, in stripes above measure, in prisons more frequent, in deaths oft. Of the Jews five times received I forty stripes save one.
>
> Thrice was I beaten with rods, once was I stoned, thrice I suffered shipwreck, a night and a day I have been in the deep;
>
> In journeyings often, in perils of waters, in perils of robbers, in perils by mine own countrymen, in perils by the heathen, in perils in the city, in perils in the wilderness, in perils in the sea, in perils among false brethren;

In weariness and painfulness, in watchings often, in hunger and thirst, in fastings often, in cold and nakedness…"

Despite his great sufferings Paul continues to say to the Galatian brethren that whatever he was able to suffer, it was not of his own power, but Christ living in him through the Holy Spirit and empowering him to stay on course.

Again, he said to the young Pastor, Timothy,

It is my personal experience that it is not easy to stay on the right path and keep going in the right direction. I have been challenged on every side and in every area of my life also, but I continue to stay committed to the Cause of God.

I recognize that I have not been; I am not; and will never be; the only one who is having a challenge in staying on course. Even Jesus prayed often in order to do so and at the time of his greatest challenge, his life under threat, he asked for his Father's help to stay on course.

The scriptures also recorded that angels have been sent to minister to him and strengthen him." We are a part of a great cause, and God has not left us alone. The Holy Spirit continues to teach us; comfort us; correct us; remind us; and empower us.

Jesus says, "Lo I am with you always." The angels of God are constantly encamped around us to deliver us out of trouble. The preceding chapters of this book are also, a source of empowerment to us. We have discussed the following:

(1) Our acceptance of Jesus as just the beginning and not the end of our journey as Christians.

(2) We experience spiritual birth in Christ Jesus and must allow our spiritual development to take place in a healthy manner.

(3) It is important for us to develop an appetite for the word of God as our spiritual source of life.

(4) That we understand the importance of the Holy Spirit in our lives.

(5) That spiritual maturity is as important as our spiritual birth and what are the indications that we are maturing as Christians.

(6) Not settling for nor content with being among the "called out" (Ecclasias) but striving always to be "chosen" (Electus).

(7) Developing spiritual self-confidence in who we are as God's chosen generation.

(8) Ensuring that our souls are at peace with God above settling for our minds to be at rest.

(9) Knowing and meeting our Christian obligations to others.

This final chapter addressing our obligations to the Cause of God is intended to serve the purpose of empowering and motivating us to commit to this great movement of God to save the world.

May we all be found worthy of our calling and be able to say that we too have fought a good fight and have finished our course.